PATTERN BEHAVIOR

The Seamy Side of Fashion

NATALIE KOSSAR

Inspired by the
**McCALL PATTERN
COMPANY'S**
Archives

WITHDRAWN

RUNNING PRESS
PHILADELPHIA

Running Press
Hachette Book Group
1290 Avenue of the Americas, New York, NY 10104
www.runningpress.com
@Running_Press

Printed in China

First Edition: October 2017

Published by Running Press, an imprint of Perseus Books, LLC,
a subsidiary of Hachette Book Group, Inc.

The Hachette Speakers Bureau provides a wide range of authors for speaking events. To find out more, go to www.hachettespeakersbureau.com or call (866) 376-6591.

The publisher is not responsible for websites (or their content) that are not owned by the publisher.

Print book cover and interior design by Ashley Todd

Library of Congress Control Number: 2017944791

ISBNs: 978-0-7624-6274-2 (print), 978-0-7624-6275-9 (ebook)

1010

10 9 8 7 6 5 4 3 2 1

I *absolutely cannot, under any circumstances, sew.*
I just can't. When I was three years old my mom's sewing cabinet
got knocked over and crashed onto me, sewing machine included.
That was my first brush with sewing and I was not impressed. Subsequent
attempts to engage with the threadly arts would prove equally disastrous.
My mom and my grandma, bless them, went to great lengths to get me to
enjoy something, anything, related to sewing. None of it took.

My mom brought me and my brother to fabric stores and encouraged
us to pick out patterns and fabrics that we liked. It was fun for a while,
but we got bored and would beg to leave. She pored over the catalogs
and pattern drawers for what felt like hours. Eventually we learned that
yarn skeins made good makeshift footballs, so we practiced our running
patterns through the aisles, pretending to be Kordell Stewart and Jerome
Bettis. He was Slash and I was The Bus.

Inspired by my yarn antics, my mom signed me up for a knitting club.
It was held on Wednesday nights and led by the Chaplain's wife. The
other girls were delighted to make complex winter hats and multicolored
washcloths. I made one cat scarf* and called it quits.

The following summer, my grandma pulled me out of a literal woodpile
to get my colors done. I reluctantly sat on the edge of her bed while she
plopped fabric swatches onto my shoulders to see what season paired
best with my complexion. She announced that I was "a summer" and
politely suggested I wear something other than my dad's military under-
shirts. I asked if I could go back outside.

So. Despite a solid effort from Mom and Grums, I simply wasn't inter-
ested in sewing. I preferred to spend my time pretending to be a horse,

* A cat-sized scarf, designed to be worn by cats.

or building forts out of scrap wood, or collecting live nightcrawlers from the backyard and feeding them to Barbles, my pet catfish. Girls who liked sewing were weak and boring. And I refused to be one of them.

Twenty years later, I got an email from my mom asking me to help her find an old sewing pattern. Like a good millennial, I took to Google and ran a quick image search. Hundreds—*hundreds*—of vintage sewing patterns flooded my computer screen, and I was instantly transported to the plastic chairs of fabric stores and running the zig-zag plays of yarn football.

Some of the images were from my mother's childhood (an era I've coined *polyesteryear*), some were from my grandma's youth, and many were from much earlier. Vintage patterns for men, women, and children dating back to the 1920's had been scanned and used as images in blogs or placed for sale—all right there online. The drawings were certainly *of a time*; demonstrating outdated social ideals of gender or race or class structure. I was both delighted and horrified by what was considered acceptable even thirty years ago. The juxtaposition of the vintage images with modern dialogue generated a strong message of social growth and change. I captioned a few of the images and sent them to a handful of friends who agreed and encouraged me to keep going.

Perhaps most importantly, the packets presented themselves in a new light. The women posed on the covers no longer seemed vapid, demure, or girly. I suddenly saw past the traditional notions of femininity—notions I spent a lifetime rejecting—and saw my foremothers as they truly were. These women were powerful. These women were complicated. These women had something to say.

So here I am, writing a book about sewing. Here I am researching a subject I once abhorred; burying myself in the patterns I couldn't escape as a kid. I am finally connecting to the world my mom and grandma share; the world they wanted to share with me since I was born. And I am glad to share in it. In my own woodpile, cat scarf, horsechild way.

Please enjoy.

—Natalie Kossar

TO MOM & GRAM & GRAMMIE & GRUMS

And to the women before us who went unheard

k. Five-Piece Skirt.
VIEW B

Hat 1227

Good hat Rose

Thank you

It keeps the pigeons off

You're just a city boy
Your pants don't even go in your shoes
Heh heh
City boy

Penny you keep that flower
You keep it all the way through college

Don't worry Rick
We'll find you someone
There's gotta be a real big lady somewhere

Oh man

I got an F on my witch test

Come catch us men
Mennn
Come get us

Patty I think

I think that's a urine sample

Do what
Remove my coat
Why
STEALING?!
Sir
Don't be ridiculous

Oh hi Cheryl

Can't talk skiing byeeee

·SEW.

DESIGNED BY:
KERSTIN MARTENSSON

Come on Blair
Do you want to pledge Chi Omega or not?

Pattern 460
Chest Sizes: 42 - 44 - 46

Men's Western
Jacket

KWIK
•SEW®

DESIGNED BY:
KERSTIN MARTENSSON

U.S. $2 50
CANADA $2 85
AUST $3 15

KWIK•SEW PATTERN CO., INC.
300 5TH AVE. NO. • MINNEAPOLIS, MINN. 55401
COPYRIGHT BY KWIK•SEW PATTERN CO., INC.

Ahhhhhh
Yep
Good day to kill a horse

Michael
Do not feed the cat a snake

Carol how hungover are you?
You forgot to wear a skirt
And you're dragging around a bag of trash

Swag hood Joyce

Hello yes we need two
Sorry DOS fajitas
Pronto
For delivery
Say Pronto
And can we get those pronto
We're knitting

Bubbles
HELL YES

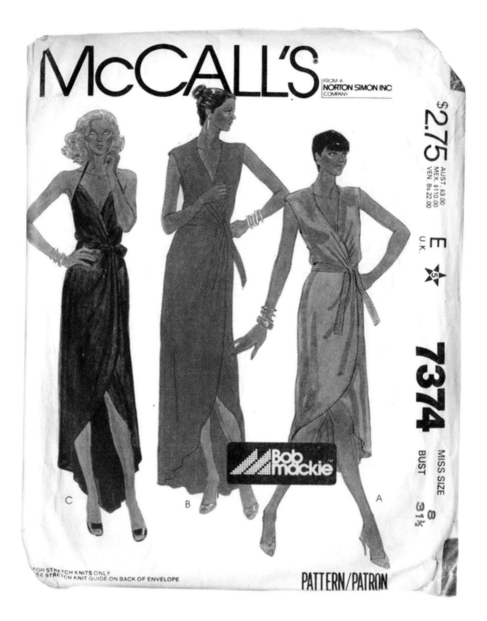

Oh wow Rita

You went blonde

No it's nice

Very natural

Shelly

Shelly come smell this leaf

There's just something about being a man
This gun knows what I'm talking about

Is that a taco
Louise?
Are there tacos?

A marlin

Doug

How am I supposed to cook a marlin?

3300

Are you a woman?
Are you dead inside?
Try Silly Hats . . .

It's a football stick
For football
Shut up Danny
You're six

So do you
Use the whole wolf
Or

On Wednesdays we wear pink

Okay Mikey here's the money
This time ask for the dank weed

Yes we like men
Why do you ask?

Yes we like women
Why do you ask?

Mr. Bear doesn't like your dress

Well Mr. Pig says your parents are getting divorced

We're actually not twins
We're triplets
But
One died

Rebecca

Did you eat that rose?

I don't dance with garbage hoes

No seriously stop talking

We'll have two vodka sodas
And a real big lady if you've got one
God Rick be cool

. . . and significantly more in-depth sexual health education. Can you help?

. . . in science but exceptional at math.
Which college programs are best?

. . . where men disrespect me. Mother says that
age lasts forever. Please advise.

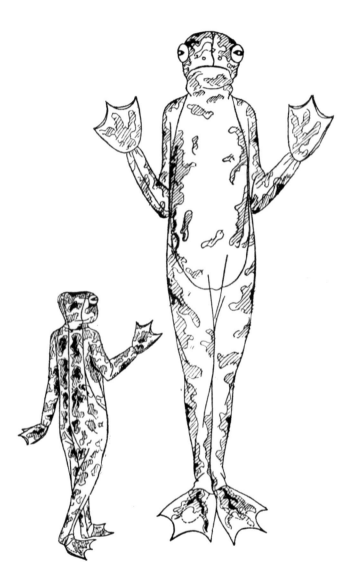

I AMPHABULOUS

This is your business card?

It just says Joan

Hey before we start

Let's just

Everyone go around and say their ages

Yes good Clara . . .

Look at Hellpocket . . .

Look at it . . .

LOOK AT IT

Haha Mr. Patterson
Mr. Patterson look
This file is big

Pssst hey
Low fives girls
I got the birth control

Helen

Where's your Moroccan robe

You're embarrassing us

A   8911   B

Haha
Take that
Ya frog

MAKE THE MOST OF YOUR INCHES

...HES count when you're on the
...t side and have hips larger than
... You want to make the most
...r height, the least of your hip
...ments. And pattern 1233 of-
...smart way to go about it.

...ree versions of this Triad have
...plicity you want first and fore-
...ext you'll notice lines that add
...r height—up and down darts in
..., clever seamings in the skirts,
...s narrow as a finger. Finally
...the subtle softness above each
...good way to minimize the hips,
...this Triad as with all the Com-
...s practical three-in-one pat-
...ach version is designed to fill a
..., your active life. There's the
... version (left) shown here in
...e rayon crepe with a feather-
...d hat (just right for your size)
...ple step-ins. There's the club-
... version (center) in wine wool
...ther small hat and long-lined
...There's the house dress (right)
...d spun rayon designed to go
...'ords that give comfort.

I wish my husband would
Am I right ladies

So fun right
Evelyn?
Hmm
This is so fun right?

No it's a nice hat

But

When will you have occasion to wear it?

Yeah Pete
We can hear you
LOUD AND QUEER
Ayyyyy
Ayyyyy

9286 Women's & Misses

Fabric Requirement

A-1

Good God Blanche

Your hand is melting

Olé

It's not tea Grace it's espresso
It's great for nerves
Very soothing

What's your birthday wish Carol?

To never see you again

Ladies' and Misses' Brim Hats

McCALL PRINTED PATTERN

375 HEADSIZE 23

35c

Adjustable ½ Inch Larger or Smaller

Are you sad?
Try Happy Hats

You were right about these capes
They do hide our teen pregnancies

Haha Jerry you scamp
That's my dick towel

Is that a Hot Pocket
Louise?
Are there Hot Pockets?

Uh oh

It's mistletoe

Someone come kiss Peggy

Or else I will

Haha

But seriously I'll kiss her

Mom come on
You're too old to trick-or-treat
Come on Mom

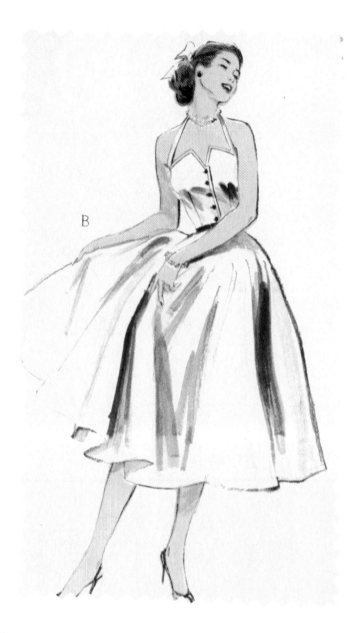

I'm married!
I'm so happy
To achieve my life goal
At nineteen

HAPPY BIRTHDAY KATE

Aw you didn't have to
Oh it's
It's buzzing

Yeah no
He definitely loves that

5928—35c

5929—45c

Oh Jan
I think you have scoliosis
Like bad

Suze

Should you be wearing platforms

You're already

You know

Big

Look
There's one right there
A black woman
She's
She's *reading*

I hope Gayle isn't coming to the party tonight . . .

Gayle just ruins everything . . .

OH HI GAYLE

Canada 70¢
Aust. & N. Z. .55, 5/6
U. K. 4/-

Hey
You're adopted

Bows and arrows at night

This sleepover rules

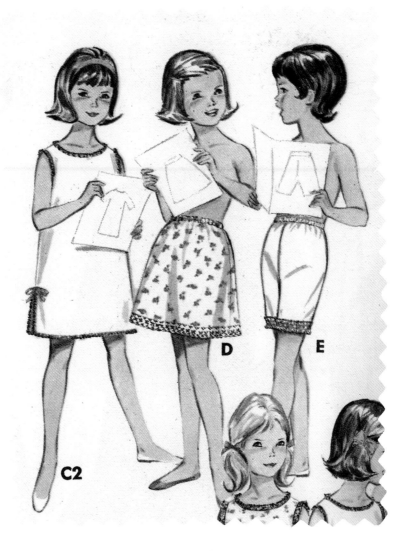

Let's all draw our panties
This sleepover blows

NIGHTY NIGHTMARES

Donna you're white
Stop saying lit

Okay girls . . .

A   B   D
C   B   E
C   B   E

Time to pick your Halloween costumes

You can be any type of girl

Go crazy!

As long as you're in a dress

Dream big.

Hey Gil and Paul this is Tom

Hi Tom I'm Gil and this is Paul and you know Bud

Hey Gil hey Paul

Hey Tom hey Bud

Tom, Paul

Bud

Paul

Marcy be honest
Does my hand look like a foot?

A   A-1

Well
Motherhood isn't for everyone

A complete calico-print transfer alphabet including three "I's"; two
[illegible] Y, Z and a ?, &, !—48 characters

I dunno man
It looks weird
WELL IT FEELS GREAT

What's with the bucket hat

Lisa?

Are you ashamed to have white friends?

Ken stop pouting
But when you said double date
I thought

This 5K is nothing
Compared to my 401K
Right Lawrence
Haha
I've never struggled

Yikes

Sharon

Can I get you a chair

Five strawberries

Five

Betsy

You were gone for an hour

Oh wow yeah

Your boyfriend sounds awful

Do you want to talk more about it

At my place

COMPANION-
BUTTERICK

B

Relax Lynn
It's just a bird
You can't get sick from birds

The hood life chose us

It's a clutch
You put little things in it
Like a mirror
Or Quaaludes

Oh you know
Dress for the job you want
What job is bear?

5356 5346

For back views see page 51.

5355. This fur-cloth coat with tuxedo revers is
est type to make. There are few pieces and they
. No   Gr

Jessica
It's just a deer
Chill

Elaine honey
Come in off the balcony
But Gary and I
Elaine
Gary died five years ago

HATS TO BEGUILE

1071   1071

Are you repulsive?
Try Beguiling Hats
Hats to beguile

6013—50c
PRINTED
PATTERN

Ugh the party last night was the worst . . .

6016—65c
PRINTED
PATTERN

At least we'll be alone for Book Club today . . .

B

A

DAMMIT GAYLE

Hey there war boy
How's the war?

I got a letter from college!
What's it say?
It says no girls allowed!
Haha
Haha

7804

Sandra pay attention
Your hot dog's on the ground

All these roosters
I still can't find a cock

Women

Am I right?

What's Cookin'?

Plan a barbecue. Friends and food are simple ingredients for fun. Be a well-dressed chef in #3988. Your apron pockets display a favorite recipe. Hers are the iron-on transfers included in the pattern.

#3625 Caftan Shirt
#4106 Embroidery
#3790 Pants

ron/mits
al Top
l Pants
ants
irt

RITE BURGERS" Shape 1 lb. ground beef into 8
Open 16 oz. can chili con carne. Put 1 table spoon

CHILI
Con
CARNE

CHILI
SAUCE

GROUND BEEF

Kevin put the bongos away
It's time for dinner

Hi
I'm Linda F.
And I have Depression

I don't want flowers
I want pants

It's fun because the popcorn is on a string
It used to be in a bowl
But now
It's on
A
String

Okay Rick

Nice and easy

Excuse me ma'am

Are you a real big lady?

Ladies Blouse
Variations

•SE

Why yes I am!

You're sure it's safe to drink
Yes Greg
But
Come on
Down the hatch

Seashells!
I hear the ocean!
TURTLEPOCKETS

Ann look at my pearls

Ann

Ann put the mirror down

No sorry
I don't do fortunes
OR DO I?
No I don't

Sharon please
Let us get you a chair

Daisy let's take off the puppets
What puppets?
These are my hands

Oh
You really had a telescope to show me
I thought
Nevermind
Yes stars are cool

Mmm yarn

1054

1053

1061

© John B. Gruelle

1063

THERE'S SOMETHING

LIKE TRIM FROCKS FOR

SUMME

She'll look like an animated si
frock, with its own bonnet (No.
blue rick rack and embroidery. Or
yoke, sleeves, and bonnet lining
frock will keep an active little tod
weather. The embroidery transfer
cluded. Sizes 6 months, 1, 2, 3 yea
dress, 1¾ yards 35-inch fabric. Co
1⅜ yards, ⅝ yard contrasting fabr

Transfer No. 1128

The three little playmates, above, are pleased with their new
frocks with the simulated smocking. The pretty diamond
effect is done in single stitch with tiny embroidered flowers.
Use this clever transfer, No. 1128, to perk up her play-
frocks, your own dirndls and blouses. Complete directions:
1⅜ yards banding, 7½ inches wide. Blue or yellow, 25c. The
three dresses shown above suggest some of the many styles
on which the embroidery may be used.

No. 1126

This little ice-cream eater likes
to be cool. Her sheer little frock
with a dash of embroidery is just
right for "dog days." The baby
puff sleeves, the sash in back win
her style vote; ease in making
wins Mother's. McCall No. 927,
sizes 1 2, 4, 6. Size 4 take- 1¾

WRONG

1 A

6

3

5
4964

4

2
4964

5064

5064

5156

...t practical of all layettes. Every-
.. a wrapped-over shirt, a slip,
..acket, cap, mittens and bootees.
.. baby easy. One size. 25c.

McCALL 5238. A little robe that buttons up snugly and
warm under its Peter Pan collar. Very few pieces to cut
out and put together. Use flannel or challis or a fleecy
cotton. Size 2, 2⅛ yards 35-inch. 5 sizes, 1-8. 25c.

WITH

TOT'S TOGS TO
FILL EVERY NEED

Dress the small-fry appropriately, and cunningly for whatever they're doing . . . playing, visiting, or when nodding with the sandman. Touches of embroidery and appliqué will make their new clothes charming and as sweet as their young lives.

Your young queen deserves a party dress like No. 1121. Make it of crisp, perky fabrics such as dimity, lawn, organdy, gingham, or percale. She'll be most fetching . . . with a big sash . . . puffed sleeves and dainty flower embroidery. The bonnet is becoming with its pert ruffle and it's made without interlining which means it is easy to iron. There's a lace edged slip to go with the dress. Sizes 6 months, 1, 2, 3 years. Size 2 requires 1¾ yards of 35-inch for dress and bonnet and ⅞ yard for slip. 5¼ yards of ⅝ inch wide lace are needed for edging on all three garments. Blue transfer for the embroidery trim. Pattern. 35 cents.

A

C

No.

No. 1121

When little-ones get ready to go to hush-a-bye land dress them in
fy, dainty igh

THE CHILDREN

Guys

GUYS GET OFF

The swing is for ONE PERSON

Your bag has such a strong odor
Like spices or
Herbs
Lois what is that?

No Roberta you hold it down here
On your hip see
Not under your chin
That's stupid

BUTTERICK
4709
Men's T-shirt, sweat pants
shorts & robe

$1.50

A

B

Well you can play but
Your friend is in a bathrobe
And lady sandals

I drew a butt!

I drew a butt too!

WE ALL DREW BUTTS

I'd swing with us

Ma'am
Quit hogging the photo booth
This is a children's party

Mom look
We found a balloon in your bedroom

Niiiiiiiice

ACKNOWLEDGMENTS

Thanks first to one hundred Nicoles;

To Nicole Tourtelot, my amazing agent at DeFiore and Company, who is sharp and cool and always knows exactly what to say. She has permission to speak on my behalf even when I am very dead.

I know what a literary agent is, Nicole.

Thanks to Nicole Chung, Nicole Cliffe, and Mallory Ortberg for being the first to agree to publish me on their brilliant website, www.the-toast.net, which is now defunct by total coincidence.

Thanks to my editor Jennifer Kasius from Running Press for taking a chance on me. And to my entire team at Running Press, for their enthusiasm and kindness. Thank you all for your patience with my technological incompetencies, which are many.

Thanks to Janet Wolfe, Stacey Long, and Meg McDonald at the McCalls Pattern Company, for agreeing to partner with me, for accommodating my research, and for making sure I wasn't locked in the closet during the fire drill.

Several people leapt at the opportunity to help me during research; Tamara Nolte graciously hosted me in Brooklyn. Maia Wynn was my dog's handmaiden and is a top-notch cohabitator. Leonard Madrid and Stephanie Graner both gave me scanners to use, and I only broke one (sorry Stef). Jayme Swalby drove me to the airport and also hit me with her car.

Thanks to my attorneys, Josiah Jenkins and Michael Powalisz, who've had my back from the beginning, and let me abuse attorney-client privilege as an excuse to talk about relationships.

Thanks to the drunken misfit weirdos in the Chicago improv/sketch community between 2006 and 2016. You developed, supported, and amplified a voice I knew existed but was afraid to use. You are my heart.

M. Molly Backes (@mollybackes) not only forged a path, but installed lights and directions along the way. She was a tireless cheerleader and validator, and I would not have made it without her.

Sarah Armstrong (@oohsarahcuda) came out of nowhere and supported me in all of the right ways. If you're working on a project—I'm telling you—you want her on it.

Robin Babb (@cixxxous) is an outstanding friend and editor (frienditor?). Thanks for the pink 100s.

Finally, my unending thanks to Alex Garday, Nathan Jansen, Eric Lindberg, Eric Muller, Leslie Nesbit, Robert Perez, Nick Semar, and Sean Sullivan, who are my muses.

And to Eileen Backes, Megan Backes, Katie Dufresne, Lisa Linke, and Jessie Stegner, who are my solid ground.